DISCLAIMER: Beautiful Soul Q⌐ poetry. This statement is included t⌐ contain strong language or subjects and should be considered for mature readers only.

Beautiful Soul
Queen Elizabeth
Shakeya E. Kinard

Beautiful Soul Queen Elizabeth

By Shakeya Kinard

Cover Art by Amber Dickerson
Created by Jazzy Kitty Publications
Logo Designs by Andre M. Saunders/Jess Zimmerman
Editor: Anelda Attaway

ISBN 978-1-7357874-2-8
Library of Congress Control Number: 2020920821

ACKNOWLEDGMENTS

To the highest of high, the God of my understanding without Him there's no me without belief nothing exist!

Thank you to my Fav Five is what I call 'em Kenyetta Coursey, Tekeisha Wilkerson, Ebony Denise, Andre Hicks (May he continue to be at peace) and Amber Dickerson. These five have been my listening ear and motivation throughout this whole process. No matter the time of day or night when I reached out they were right there with nothing but great feedback.

To my beautiful children for staying patient and understanding while mommy wrote or needed a moment of peace. I love you to life!

To my amazing mother (Jackie Kinard) just for being exactly who she is; her strong independence and drive to succeed at life is what gives me all the strength I need.

A special thank you to Mrs. Jazzy Kitty my publisher cause without her we wouldn't be reading this. I'm forever grateful and can't wait to see what kinda magic we can create!

Thank you Jerry Toston for providing with information to get my book off the ground. Everyone I reached out to turned their back on me. So I'm extremely thankful for your kindness, Peace and blessings to you.

ACKNOWLEDGMENTS

To my special friend who on many of days would not let me give up. He played a major part in uplifting and inspiring me to do better in life no matter what! Love you always G.G.

Last but definitely not lease, my host of Facebook friends and family. When I say you guys rock, I mean that from the bottom of my heart! From the jump, you guys were on deck with everything I posted; giving me the motivation and drive to continue writing. I love you all and I mean that with my whole heart!

DEDICATIONS

This book is dedicated to special people; Taylor Omer'e Gardner and Ayce Omar Gardner; The Star of the Universe and The Highest Spade in any Deck! My Forever Loves.

TABLE OF CONTENTS

TABLE OF CONTENTS

INTRODUCTION

Just like everyone else in the world, we all got a story to tell whether others can relate or not. Sometimes just to talk about it or better yet, read about it brings some type of relief to our lives. There are people struggling in the world every day due to different issues like Depression, Love, Accomplishments, Heartbreak, Sexual or Physical Abuse, Beliefs, Domestic Violence, or Death! Most people if they're anything like me don't like to talk about it. So to read about somebody else with the same struggles kind of makes us feel a little better about what we're going through in life!

Everyone has a path or a pass in life; what's yours?

How did you deal with it?

What did you do to overcome it?

Many people are still dealing with these issues but are too afraid to open up due to the world's stereotypes and judgmental people.

Beautiful Soul Queen Elizabeth is definitely a book that everyone can relate to, male or female. I'm a living testimony to everything written in this book. I pray that those of you that are still sick and suffering; this book will bring you some type of strength! This is just the beginning for Queen Elizabeth, so be on the lookout.

A BAD ONE

Beauty is more than SKIN DEEP

When will a person learn a GOOD HEART

And GOOD LOOKS

CAN'T COMPETE

She can be a 10 on the OUTSIDE

But a 3 DEEP Within

All she knows is her Looks

And how to Play the TYPICAL MEN!

The Ones who think a NICE Body and Face

Means they WIN

But the Minute they get to Know her

It will QUICKLY END!

ATTITUDE OUT OF CONTROL

Pouting like she's 10-years-old

All-cause you told her NO

And she CAN'T HOLD her own!

You're her SOLE PROVIDER
And all she knows is to be Cute
Sis, don't even know the Difference between
A Sky and the Color Blue

But you think you're Winning
Better get a REAL WOMAN
And START a New Beginning
Someone who wants for Nothing
But always Providing you with Something!

She got her Own and wouldn't call Tyrone
Help you to be Better
Without even Hearing that Word
With the L Letter!

A Solid Situation
And wouldn't care who was Hating
At End of the Day
You're the One she's Dating

When REAL FEELINGS are Involved

You can't help but to LOVE

But all that FAKE SHIT

Will have you Wearing an OJ GLOVE!

Looks or Real know the Difference!

ALONE

They say ALONE makes you Strong

But they NEVER said it Would Feel Like This

I don't know if I'm Losing

Or if I Controlling this Shit

Mind Racing

While My Heart constantly Pacing

Hands Shaking

I don't know if I Can Take It!

Crying to my God

Like it has to get Better

Don't know what I should do

Maybe write Him a Letter

Tell Him how I Feel

And PRAY He ALLOWS me to Heal

Cause this Weight on my Shoulders

Is like Carrying Bricks up a Hill

There's NO Pill
That's gone Seal this Deal
I wannabe Nourished
And FULL like a Thanksgiving Meal

One Big Happy Family
Is ALL I ask for
Like Jordan hitting a 3 Pointer
In the Final Four!!!

The Crowd goes Wild
And all we can do is Smile
Thank you, God for it has been
A LONG WHILE

Peace and Blessings
This has DEFINITELY been a Lesson
But Never let family go ALONE
While Stressing!

Embrace them and Love them

And NEVER let any Harm be done!!!

For you Never know them Tables Can Turn

And then You'll be the One

But best believe when you Call family

They Gonna Come

With NO Hesitation

Like a Smoking Gun!!!

*Cherish them while they can Smell

Their Flowers!!!

Queen Elizabeth ♡

A SECRET NOT KEPT

This Creeping Shit is getting Old

And things are about to Unfold

How you gonna act

When your SECRETS are Exposed?

Shocked or Surprised?

Or better yet, Planning Your Demise

Cause you know, once I Talk

You can't Cover up the Lies!

You living Two Lives

And can NO LONGER Hide

Why keep me in Disguise?

When I'm an Award-Winning Prize!!!

Not meant to be kept a SECRET

Especially when most Guys only get a Hi and Bye

I should be put on a Pedestal

And Praised like the Gods in the Skies

Worshiped and Catered
To give me a Natural High

Why have Cake?
When I'm a homemade Sweet Potato Pie
The kind your Grandmother used to Bake
Without making a Mistake!

NOTHING Store Brought
But made from Scratch
How you got a Piece of Heaven
And Don't Know How to Act?

Better take Heed and Step up and Lead
Before time RUNS OUT
Leaving you to Plead

Not the 5th but for All the Right Shit
Leaving ALL Your Baggage
Cause I'm NOT Having It!

A SECRET was Enough

Now umma Call Your Bluff

You either IN THIS or OUT

However, it Turns Out

Just make sure you're Willing

To EXCEPT the Words Coming Out Your Mouth!

One False Move

And I'm Leaving you to Choose

Just make the Right Decision

Cause we BOTH Can't Lose

NEVER WAS A SECRET

BUT AN ABSOLUTELY KEEPER

Take a Look at the LINE

Standing BEHIND her

And that's just the Guys

Who are WAITING to MEET HER!!!!

Some Women have a NATURAL VIBE!

BEST FRIEND

We've been through Hell and Back
And NEVER Cracked

You're my to my LEFT
And I'm your LEFT to your Right
And anytime things Went Down
WE WERE READY TO FIGHT!!!

Parties all over
Many Drunken Nights
Sometimes not making it Home
Till it was Daylight

So many Memories and Moments
That NEVER made it to Light
Cause they are our Secrets
That I'll KEEP for Life!

When I had Heartbreak
You were there
Causing Hell on ANYONE
Leaving NOTHING to Spare!

I LOVE YOU MORE is what we Say
And STILL, nobody Understands till this Day!
Keep them Snakes Away, that's how we Played
Never allowing others to COME OUR WAY!

It was ALWAYS all Fun and Games
And we Still Remain
Many a night, we Rock Out like we INSANE
And I Love you like NO OTHER
And I know you'd Say the Same!

Cause you're the BEST to my FRIEND
And I'm the Friend to Your Best
No need to Continue on people, you Know the Rest
MY BEST IS YOUR BEST!!!

BLACK MAN

Nothing in Life can change

This Beautiful Sight

So Strong, So Ambitious, So Handsome

AND MY TYPE

Just the Thought of you

Gets Me Hype

God, PLEASE Let me Hold onto this Man

With ALL my Might

Sending Chills All Over

While Feeding my Mind, Body, and Soul

This Feeling I have could NEVER get Old

Caressing me from my Temples

To My Toes

It's like I Hit the Jackpot

And FOREVER I'm Sold

MY BLACK KING

MY EVERYTHING

I pray to the HEAVENS this is not a Dream

Or apart of a Movie I NEVER SEEN!!

His World, His Safe Haven,

His Nubian Queen

I plan to make his Life Amazing

And Our Reality

All Your Wants and ALL Your Needs

Will be my Pleasure, MY BLACK KING

So Request away as I'll approve whatever

Just to have you in My Life FOREVER

God Protect Our BLACK KINGS

Queen Elizabeth ♡

BOY MOM

Son is the most Sweetest Word

To ever come Outta a Mommy Face!

The Love is Something Unconditional

It's NO WORDS to even Explain!

He does NO WRONG in our Eyes

They're SO SWEET Like

TASTYKAKE'S SWEET APPLE PIE!

He gets AWAY with Murder

As if he was to COMMIT ONE

I'd turn into LAW and ORDER

A whole Detective and Investigator

Cause NOBODY comes Between that LOVE

For Mama and her Baby!

His Smile means EVERYTHING

And his Voice WARMS my Heart

NOBODY can ever Tear this BOND APART

Teach him his Worth also Responsibilities

Cause WHOEVER gets his Heart

MUST PLAY for Keeps!

Mommy always says, May the Best Person Win

Cause no matter our Love, Won't End!

Keep him Safe and Raise him Well

He has NO CHOICE but to Excel

As he Grows, he will Pull Away

But them Memories with his Mama

He will ALWAYS Replay!

AYCE GARDNER

THANK YOU FOR MAKING ME A BOY MOM!!

BROKEN WOMEN

What started out as a Fling

Opened my Eyes some AMAZING Things

Never experienced Love at First Sight

Until after that Night

For 6 months

Constituency was EVERYTHING

Wasn't until the 7th month

I noticed the Change in Me

You've been in my Bed

In and Out my Personal Life

Around my Kids, me around Yours

And Yet, I'm NOT Your Wife

You play this ROLE, Oh So Well

That now, I've Fallen HEAD OVER HILLS

Insecurities start to Appear

Now, I'm questioning Who, What and Where

Whole Time I'm just a Fling

Just SOMETHING to Do

In the Midst of his

In-Between

Now, I hear that SAME SOUND

From years ago

You Deserve what you're Worth

What have I done to Deserve this Hurt?

When I gave you my Heart

After Not Knowing if this was for

Better or Worse

Should've KNOWN Better since

I was the Other Chick

But this is to be Expected

When a person saying

ALL THE RIGHT SHIT

I say all this to say

NEVER TRUST a man who's Cute

Funny and has great DICK!

Regardless of how it Became

The PAIN is Still the Same

Heartbreak is a BITCH

But KARMA is her Middle Name!

SK ✌️

BUM ISH

Oh, you Think you're FINER

Cause Dressed up in them

High Price Designers,

News Flash THAT SHIT IS MINOR!!

Show me a Policy

Nowadays, that's like you hit the Lottery

Bury me with NO GOFUND ME

And make sure my kids Live Life Tax-Free!

Priorities all FUCKED UP

You think a Bad Bitch or Nigga mean

You Lucked up

More like get CHA BUCKS UP!

INVEST IN YOU

Stop FOCUSING on what you can Do

To down the next

Shit play outright you might can

CUT SOME CHECKS!

Have your NAME on Something

Other than a Chain or Earrings

What's that's gone Prove

But some CHUMP CHANGE!

Going out and Partying

But come home to a One Room Inn

Better known as Your Moms or Pops House

WHAT'S THIS ALL BOUT?

Nah, that's not Wavy

More like Brown Ass Water

Or some Weak Ass Gravy!

Umma need you to do Better

As a Man and Lady!

SET EXAMPLES AND GOALS

For these PRECIOUS Babies

CONFUSED

One MINUTE we are Cool

Then the NEXT I'm Confused

I don't like this Feeling

So it's time for Some Ground Rules

Never wanna keep me Guessing

Cause then, I'll grab my Bat

And Show you who's Catching

You know, I'm the Coach

And I'll TEACH you a Lesson

Have you Walking around asking God

What did I do to deserve this BLESSING?

You EITHER In or Out

But it's a MUST we see what this is About

Cause I don't want NO Man

Whoever has Doubts

LIFE TO SHORT to be Wasting Time

Plus, these dudes coming out of Nowhere

Like a Jordan Release Day Line

He said my MOUTH IS SLICK

But Damn you Thick

Asked him, have you ever Tasted

A HUMAN SNICKER?

Cause if Not

You gotta be Quicker

For every Line, I had a Timely Response

Play with them LITTLE BITCHES

Cause I'm NOT the One

I'm here for a Great Time

While having Fun

Please DON'T Blow Me Away

Like a SMOKING GUN

Now he's Standing there

LOOKING CONFUSED

Cause the Roles have Changed

I'm Sorry, did you Forget my LAST NAME???

I'm ones of the REALIST left

In this Day & Age

And let's Forget to Mention

I'M SELF MADE!!!

Talk to me, NICE

Cause Playing me

Is like SHOOTING DICE 🎲

Queen Elizabeth ♡

CRUSH OR BE CRUSHED

Should I Speak?

Or let him Pass Me By?

After all,

He DOESN'T know I'm Alive!

Scared to make the FIRST MOVE

So I continue to Play Everything Cool

Just don't wanna Mess Up

AND FEEL LIKE A FOOL!

My Nerves ALWAYS get the Best of Me

And I Automatically FREEZE

I don't know if this is a Test

Or My Mind Playing Tricks On Me!

I notice him STARING

But I'm not sure if it's for the Same Reason

You know sometimes People come into your Life

AT DIFFERENT SEASONS

And it's usually to LEARN A LESSON
Sometimes even to Receive a Blessing
I JUST DON'T KNOW WHAT TO DO
And now I'm Stressing!

Do I Approach him?
Or Wait to See if he Comes for Me?
Is this Knot in my Stomach telling me
TO LET IT BE?

Or is it BUTTERFLIES telling me
He's my HUSBAND to be!?

At this point, I Just Don't Know
If I could have it My Way
He'd be RESPONSIBLE for this Glow!

We'd be Perfect for Each Other
With the RIGHT AMOUNT of Balance
But that goes to say
If You Will Allow It!

We can take TRIPS

And go on EXPENSIVE DATES

Lay Around and Be Great

I can see a FUTURE with you as my Mate

I just Hope I OVERCOME my Fear

BEFORE IT'S TOO LATE!

SPEAK UP OR GET LEFT BEFORE IT STARTS!

DEPRESSION

It's really a Disease

Yet, we are to Ashamed to Express our Needs!

We Shut Down, Lash Out and Isolate

From what we think are our Enemies

It's People who Talk about it

And make Jokes about it

When for the Person who's Suffering

IT'S NO FUN!

It's Like Staring Down the Trigger

Of a Loaded Gun

Ready for the War in your Head to End

That's Already Begun

It's SO MANY Demons

Not Only One!

How can People NOT know

Especially when all the ACTIONS SHOW

NO LIFE, NO LIGHT
Just ALL Misery
A person can Only Take So Much
Before they START THINKING UNCLEARLY!

We have to start asking QUESTIONS
No matter the Consequences
YOU NEVER KNOW-HOW
Or WHAT that Person is Missing

A WARM Smile, a GENUINE Heart
It's the Little Things that go very far
Something Simple helps
Even if it wasn't INTENTIONAL

It can be what a person NEEDS
To get through a SERIOUS Issue
Stop biting your TONGUE
Which I'm sure is NOT Fun

And be that One who

HELPS ANOTHER

And END the Disease

Called DEPRESSION!

I'M A SURVIVOR

DIFFERENT STROKES

First comes SUNDAY

He wants the MEAL and the BODY RUB

Next, There's MONDAY

THE WINE DOWN

And Wanna Talk about the Future Type

Then We have TUESDAY

THE TURN-UP

And ALWAYS Wanna See You Type

Of course, It's WEDNESDAY

That HUMP DAY type that's POSSESSIVE

And always Wanna Fight

Here comes THURSDAY

THE DATE NIGHT TYPE

The get you Ready for

The Weekend Pipe

Followed by FRIDAY

The Party with taking Selfies

For Instagram and Facebook-type

Last but not least, there's SATURDAY

THE ONE WHO GOT YOU OPEN

Yet, you're ALWAYS Nervous

The One you Could See yourself With

But he's NOT

WILLING TO COMMIT!

I say all this to say,

Men play, but Women play BETTER

Never give 'em the Upper Hand

Cause that's NEVER APART of the Plan

They Dealt the Hand

But they ALSO got Played

Be careful of others Feelings

Cause that's when Hands Get Laid

But that's when the One

You Once CALLED KING

Get REPLACED by his Ace of Spade ♠

CALLED YOUR BLUFF!!!!

DOMESTICS

How can you HARM something

That's so Special to you

How can you HURT someone

THAT'S SO LOYAL?

Your Words ALONE

CUT DEEP

It's No Need to Beat me!

You Punch on me

Like I'm a PUNCHING BAG

Yet, you want to Cover it up

When Someone Asks!

As if the Black Eyes aren't Enough

You Rape me REPEATEDLY

To Shut Me Up

Body Bruise Badly
And you Jump at any Chance
YOU GET TO GAG ME

What have I Done
That's So Wrong?
Why do CONTINUOUSLY
Break My Bones?

The World sees my Cries
And they Pray for your DEMISE
But it's up to me to Say Goodbye!

Love DOESN'T Hurt
But what do you do
When Love doesn't Work?

Give up Start Over
And Hope you NEVER need
ANOTHER SHOULDER?

To Cry On that is Only
To be taken Advantage of
It's a Repeated Cycle
That I CHOOSE NOT to Recycle!

I'm NOTHING like you
Yet, I choose to Stay and Fight for you
Didn't think you would, Wanna
TAKE MY LIFE TOO!

In the Beginning, you LOVED me
But maybe I was too Blind to See

I guess the Plan was NEVER to Wife me
Just USE me and ABUSE me
AND TO MAKE A FOOL OF ME

Eventually, I got the Strength to Leave
After Dropping to my Knee
Begging my Lord to HELP ME PLEASE!

My Life FLASHED BEFORE my Eyes

And it was then I knew

If I didn't Get Away

I would DIE at the Hands of YOU!

Domestic Abuse is NEVER the way

And I'll go to my GRAVE Telling My Story

If it means another woman

Lives to See ANOTHER DAY!

SPEAK OUT OR SCREAM WHICHEVER WORKS!

ECSTASY

All I could do was Yell

GOD!

As I RELEASED not only

Emotionally but Physically

I QUESTIONED...

How is it Possible?

How do you Work My Body

Like an Obstacle Course

I'll NEVER Know

But at this Point, I'll NEVER GO!!

WIDE OPEN

NOT Slightly Cracked

And the thought of LOSING you

GIVES ME A PANIC ATTACK

Out here FEENING like a Junkie

Searching for Some Crack!

Whole-time I'm Singing

I WANT MY BABY BACK BABY BACK!

Oh Yeah,

That sound like Bars,

BUT THIS IS REAL

THIS NIGGA GOT ME TRIPPING

BUT IT'S REALLY HOW I FEEL

Y'all know like the Saying,

IF LOOKS COULD KILL

Might as well GO HEAD

And Write the Will

Cause I'm Locked in a

I'LL LET THIS BITCH SPILL

ANTI VIOLENCE
So I'm not talking Drama
I'm talking bout this Lil Baby
That I call PHAT MAMAS!!!

Super Soaker
You the Type that makes you wanna Choke
But then you Realize she ain't Fucking wit
NO AVERAGE JOKER!!!

SPOILED HER
Now you don't know what to do
DON'T LOSE FOCUS
And ALWAYS Stay True

But MAKE SURE you
HIT HER OFF
Cause we don't want to Hear,
IT'S THE END FOR YOU!!!

*WISE DECISION

Will KEEP you Around

But Staying True

WILL KEEP YOU SANE!!

Queen Elizabeth ♡

EMOTIONAL CREATURES

They say WOMEN Cheat Best

But I'm about to put this

SHIT TO REST

Unstable Creatures

YES

But that's only after you

Put us through SO MUCH MESS!

Catering to your EVERY Need

So there's NO CHEATING In Between

ONLY to Be LET DOWN

AND CRYING ON OUR KNEES

NOW WE'RE SCORN

Walking Around with Smoke

Coming outta our Heads

Like a RAGING BULL with Horns

Now we're Crazy and Out-Of-Control

Because you Acted off some Sexual Emotions

YOU COULD NOT HOLD

NOW THAT'S BOLD!

And you definitely Broke the Code

But watch how I Turn up

On some SAVAGE MODE

NOW THERE'S 1 AND 2

And NO MORE

Now I'm about to Treat these 2

HOW I SHOULD HAVE DONE YOU

Now, I'm a Hoe

And so Freaking Joe

But what you're saying about that, Dude

THOUGHT HE WAS YOUR BRO?

Unfortunately, you Lost

Now I got A BOSS

Long story short, if you gonna Cheat,

CHEAT WITH A CAUSE

Never LEAVE your Wife for a CHICK

You're only gonna have for One Night

Cause in the End

SHE'S GONE WIN WITHOUT A FIGHT!!!

Queen Elizabeth ♡

ETERNITY

Tingling ALL OVER at just the Sight

Come over here, I DON'T BITE

Spoke Softly and So Polite

CHILLS ALL OVER MY BODY

And the thought was so Nice

The Things I Would Do

If we just had ONE NIGHT

ONE NIGHT

To Explore each other's Insides

Take you to ECSTASY

At the HIGHEST HEIGHT

Just ONE NIGHT

TO GET IT ALL RIGHT

And I PROMISE to Hold you

EXTRA TIGHT

Music Playing, Candles lit,

Aroma Smelling Amazing

And My Lingerie SUPERFIT

TO TOP IT

The Strawberries are so Ripe

And READY to be Sucked

Kinda like your PIPE

Kissing and Licking

ALL OVER YOUR BODY

Has me EXTREMELY Hype

The MEMORIES will be Forever Lasting

FROM THIS ONE NIGHT

Breathing HEAVILY cause

I'm Super Excited and ready to Blow

But I must COMPOSE myself cause

I NEED YOU TO KNOW

It's ALL About you

IN THIS MOMENT

So Lay Back and be my Opponent

I want TOTAL CONTROL

So I know you're gonna

EXPLODE

Let me APPRECIATE your Canvas

For what it is

Let me VISUALIZE this Masterpiece

And Create what is Meant To Be

EVERLASTING!!!

EVERY GREAT THING COMES WITH TIME!!!

Queen Elizabeth ♡

EXPOSE ME

You can't EXPOSE me

Because the World knows me

I'm an OPEN BOOK

TRUTH BE TOLD B

Call me a HOE

But That's OLD B

NOTHING YOU CAN SAY

That's the OLD ME!

We all have a PASS

But this FUTURE I have

Is telling you TO KISS MY A**!

You can't HOLD ME DOWN

Even CLOWN me

If you ask me, your Best Bet is

TO CROWN ME!

Been through TOO MUCH
To ALLOW you to Defeat
Or even Critique Me!

Back in the Day
You COULDN'T EVEN get me to Speak!
Now, I'm on My New Me
I CAN'T BE BEAT!

Walk A MILE in my Shoes
You would Rather be KILLED
It's like walking up a NEVER ENDING HILL
In a Stiletto Heel

YOU WILL LOSE
Cause you AIN'T as Strong as me
I Climbed the Highest Mountain
ON BENDING KNEE!

I don't need a REWARD for being me
I LOVE who I'm, and that's the KEY
TO EVERLASTING HAPPINESS
And Life WITHOUT Defeat!

Live, Laugh, Love, and REPEAT!

FAMILY TIDES

Through Thick and Thin

WE IN IT TO WIN

It's NO COMING Between Us

CAUSE WE ROCKING TILL THE END!

Compete, Sneak, Diss

Do WHATEVER you want

Just know when we come

We coming as ONE

Not asking NO questions

Not EVEN Fussing

Just when we get there

It's gone be SOME HEAD BUSSING!

This Blood Running through our Veins

Is a Family Tree that's been

HURT WITH PAIN!

We can't Afford ANYMORE UPSETS
That's why we Bury any Questions
AND PUT THEM TO REST!

It was always 10 OR BETTER
To One House
And when we made our PRESENCE
It was ALWAYS Quiet as a Mouse

Nobody Turned
Or Said Anything
Cause they Knew we were Riding
For the Smallest Thing!

One Swing
We ALL Swing
Wasn't Picking sides
WE WERE ALL ON ONE TEAM!

If Grandma said Move

Best Believe we had Something to PROVE

And the ONE THING we Knew

WAS NOT TO LOSE!

If ONE Lost, We ALL Lost

And we weren't Taking that at ANY Cost!

As Big Mama would say

IT COST TO BE THE BOSS!

INSEPARABLE

Is what we're Known for

So if ANYTHING comes to Light

Just know we SETTLING the Score!

THICK AS THIEVES NO IN BETWEEN!

FAVORITE PASTIME

When I want to ESCAPE

I PICK up a Pen

And let the Words FIND

THEIR PLACE

ALONG THE LINES

I leave WHATEVER comes to Mind

It's really my Favorite

PASTIME

A No Judgement Zone

A Place to CALL Home

And Feel at Peace

When I'M ALL ALONE

Expressing my Feelings and Thoughts

NOT AFRAID TO READ

THE RESULTS!

It's whatever is INSIDE ME

At the Point in Time

It's like the Blind Leading the Blind

But the WORDS come out SURPRISINGLY Fine

Never know what you're CAPABLE OF

Just gotta be Certain

TO DO WHAT YOU LOVE!

You can be Good at whatever

But if it means NOTHING to you

It really just Something to Do

Good Days, Sad Days, even Bad Days

But with a PEN IN HAND

I'M GLAD ALWAYS!

FOLLOW YOUR HEART

No matter how long it TAKES YOU TO START!

FRIEND/ENEMY

They CLAIM they're Looking out for you

Whole-time they really Doubting you

SMILING IN YOUR FACE

When they KNOW, that's the Case

FAKING A FRIENDSHIP

Meanwhile, LATER

They're DEMOLISHING it

They say the Grass is Greener

But NEVER said

IT WAS SNAKES IN IT!

Taking all your Vulnerable Moments

And using them to EXPOSE you

Not knowing that's the Last Straw

CAUSING ME TO HURT YOU

They say Two Wrongs

DON'T make a Right

But they NEVER said...

I couldn't Beat your Ass in a Fight

LOVE OR HATE

Either way, it's a Checkmate

For a Friend to SMILE in your Face

Knowing she was a FAKE BITCH

Truth always comes out

IN THE END

That's why our Parents always wanna

PICK OUR FRIENDS

We be MAD as Shit

But it always Turns out to Be Legit

FAKE BITCHES MAKE ME SICK

Smile in your Face

THE WHOLE TIME

And will Straight up Snitch (Rip Dirt)

You may Come Across

A FEW REAL ONES

And Later they become Ya Day 1's

But Trust

You'll NEVER have to worry about

NOT PULLING THE GUN

They gonna Ride

To the WHEELS FALL OFF

And Let NO HARM be Done

But you gotta know How to Separate

The Fake Friends

FROM YA REAL ONES!!!

KEEP YA GRASS CUT
AND THIS TO SHALL PASS!!

Queen Elizabeth ♡

GAVE YOU THE BEST OF ME

From SUNUP to SUNDOWN
I Treated you as if you Walked Around
WITH A CROWN!

You were My King
My Reality and NOT a Dream
You know, like the Dude
In Coming to America, HAKEEM!

I was your Queen to be
And I Worshiped you like
THE AMERICAN DREAM

Only to be Treated like
SCUM and a DIRTY BUM!
Someone you wouldn't give TWO CENTS too
Or even BREADCRUMBS!

What Part of the Game is that?

You know God DON'T like Ugly

So it's DEFINITELY GONNA BE Payback

Just don't know When

Or how you should React

But don't say I didn't WARN you

WHEN YOU FEEL THE IMPACT!

You do things to Hurt me PURPOSELY

But what will you Do

Once the PAIN ERUPTS from ME?

I'M NOT RESPONSIBLE FOR

WHAT PAIN I CAUSED TO YOU

As you DIDN'T Care

When you were the One

Wearing the Shoe!

Women get off for

INSANITY

I Wonder if My LUCK is as Good

As I Hoped it would be

PRAY FOR ME

To Change this Mind Frame

I have Cause at ANY GIVEN Moment

I'M ABOUT TO SPAZZ!

Call WHOEVER you Want

Cause at this Given Moment

They're most likely

GONNA PASS

You think What you Want

But the Fun has just Begun

If I make ONE PHONE CALL

THIS WILL ALL BE DONE!

I'm Sparing you cause

I ONCE Cared for you

But don't ever let this Beautiful Heart

Cloud what can Bury you!

A BROKEN HEART SCORN

Could EASILY be the End for You!

GIRL DAD

Best Daddy in the World
IS WHAT I WOULD CALL HIM
Raised me like his Own
And DIDN'T EVEN Birth Me!

NEVER TOLD ME NO
And Kept me in the Latest
Always made it known
I was his FAVORITE!

Stepped up to the Plate
And was ALWAYS on Time
NEVER LATE

Showed me what Life was about
And how I SHOULD be Treated
IF I EVER DECIDED TO DATE!

Made me FEEL like a Princess

Amongst ALL BOYS

Just the FEELING of being LOVED

BROUGHT ME SO MUCH JOY

SPOILED

Was an UNDERSTATEMENT

Can't be Matched

OR ANOTHER REPLACEMENT!

My LOVE for my Daddy

Is a LOVE that INDESCRIBABLE

The LOVE I have for MINE

IS UNDENIABLE

SO I CAN DEFINITELY RELATE

And I PRAY they Live Longer than Me

FOR GOD'S SAKE!

His only Daughter

His only Ruler

And I couldn't ask for another Dad

THAT'S COOLER

Keeps me on my Toes and Under Control

If he EVER NEEDED a Heart

CONSIDER MINE SOLD!

Daddy's Only Girl!!

GIRL MOM

Princess DESCRIBES her Best!

And I'm her Queen

SO YOU KNOW THE REST!

She is LITERALLY My Best Move

IN THE GAME OF CHESS

And at the End of the Day

She is my GREATEST Success

My Story that is Cause WITHOUT her

IT'S NO LIFE TO LIVE!

Strong-Willed and a Beautiful Personality

She Reminds me a lot of MY YOUNGER ME

Smile that LIGHTS UP the Room

And Good at WHATEVER she do

She makes the Impossible

Look Possible Effortlessly

I Swear she is really a MINI ME!

So INDEPENDENT to the Point it Scares me

I just Hope the man who is Blessed with her

CAN HANDLE A QUEEN B!

She can be a LONER sometimes

But ALONE MAKES YOU STRONG

But it doesn't Define her Exterior at all

She so Lovely and Flawless

She can OWN any Room

WITH HER GRACEFULNESS

And her CHOCOLATE SKIN!

BRAINS amongst BEAUTY

That's her Biggest Asset

She gonna RUN the World with the Best

AND THAT CAN CONFESS!!!

TAYLOR OMER'E IS THE REASON

I'M A GIRL MOM!

GUY FLIRTS

They say all the RIGHT THINGS

To get you Excited

Only cause they think the Goal

Will be to ENTICE you

Buy you Expensive Gifts

And take you on Trips

Not for you Tho

Only for his KICKS!

Thinking with his LITTLE HEAD

And not his Big Head

He gonna Wish to God

HE DID

When he finds out

All the STUFFED HE DID

Was him Making his OWN Bed

To Lay IN Of Course

BUT NOT WITH A WARM BODY

More like a Poor Sport

Because she Knew from the Jump

It wasn't Going Down

NOW SHE A CLOWN

And you Left Broke

Shoulda knew better

When you TRIED to Play her

LIKE A JOKE!

Every Female is not EASILY Impressed

With Money that is Could of Just

Came to the TABLE AS IS!

AND THAT'S YOUR BEST!

Being yourself WILL get you Further

THAN YOU THINK

Cause Dealing with a Queen

She Gonna Uplift a King!

CHECKMATE AT ITS BEST!

HUMBLE BEE

HUMBLE is all I know how to be

Don't Speak that SHIT to me

After all, I came up in the Dirt

THE STREETS OF 3B

3rd and Broom, to be exact

You know where the REAL NIGGAS

And HITTERS be at!

TALK SHIT TO THEIR SIS

They're gonna Push Ya Wig Back!

Have you Rethinking

Like DAMN, why I do that?

NO OUTSIDERS ALLOWED

That's How I was ALWAYS Taught

So if I ACT Real Bougie

IT AIN'T MY FAULT!

No Limit to it

And all we know is to Do It

AIN'T NO EXCUSES

And Nigga we TRUE to This!

Copping Pleas and Wanna Plead the 5th

Take this ASS WHOOPING like a Gangster bish!

Did you think they were gonna

Let you GET AWAY with this Shit?

Unlike other Folks

Mines show me the Upmost

So they ain't letting NOTHING come between us

WITHOUT NO SMOKE!

So you Play like it a JOKE

FOR KINFOLK

But Know it's gone End

CUTTHROAT

Now I'm gonna keep this one Brief

Because I ALREADY went to Deep

Just Keep in Mind NEVER WANNA FUCK

WITH A SISTER FROM 3B!

HYPOCRITICAL WOMEN

To Laugh at ANOTHER WOMEN'S Hurt

As she's going THROUGH her Sorrow

IS LOW

Especially when your TIME

IS BORROWED

You don't have to Put yourself

IN HER SHOES

Cause it's a Time in ALL WOMEN Lives

WHERE THIS WILL BE YOU

EMBRACE HER

Tell her to PICK HER CROWN UP

Tell her She Got This

GRAB HOLD of your Sister

And Ensure her that

WE ALL HAVE OUR PICKS

This Pain WILL hit Deep

But it's up to you

Whether you SWIM or SINK

Remember who you are

And Bury these SCARS

This by far has been the hardest Battle

But you are Amongst some BRIGHT STARS

Women with Goals, Careers

And Ambitions

Never settle for a Man you don't want

In your Kitchen

Words to the Wise

Spread your Wings

YOU WILL FLY HIGH!!

It's FEELS So Much Better

When you WALK WITH PRIDE

LESSONS LEARNED

That's a Part of Life

But being an AMAZING WOMAN

YOU WILL FIGHT! FIGHT! FIGHT!!!

But NEVER Alone

Because your Sisters got your Back

And this Love we have for you

Is bad to the Bone

So you will NEVER Lack

UPLIFT YOUR SOUL SIS,

AND YOU WILL WIN!!!

Queen Elizabeth ♡

LIL' BABY

Heavy on the Love

Is the ONLY THING I can Think of

When YOU come to Mind

Because it's the ONLY THING I knew

To Show you at the Time

You were my Everything

AND MORE

And Everything you Did

I TRULY ADORED

But this Hurt you Showed me

IS A PAIN

I'd Wish it on NO ONE

It's like being Held Up at Gun Point

And Nowhere to Run!

I gave you Literally

EVERYTHING thing I had

And you Threw it Away

Like TRASH from a Dump Truck

QUESTIONING MYSELF

Time and Time AGAIN

Like, what have I Done?

Where have I Been?

I NEVER Betrayed you

More like a Slave for you!

Would do Anything in the World

To AMAZE you

Yet, I got Played too

Never know what Kinda Games

People have for you

They Show you their
TRUE COLORS
And Leave you Singing the Blues

Like Damn I Snoozed
SO I GUESS I LOSE

Boo Boo the Fool,
That's ALL I keep Hearing
Nothing really matters
Cause NO ONE Cares!!

They just Wanna Know
So they can Hear
I TOLD YOU SO

He was Just like the Rest
Yet, You Gave him your Best!!!

Yes, the Best parts of me

And if he EVER Calls

I'll go Running

Cause I Loved him

With EVERYTHING in me

WILL FOREVER BE!

LOST

YOU SNOOZE YOU LOSE
Or whatever they Call it
By the End of this Game
It ain't gone be NO RULES
IT'S OVER!

Talk that HEAVY SHIT
Cause we all know
You Making up for that Limp

You know SMOKE SOME LEAN
Pop a Perk, Drink some Remy
YOU DID ALL THAT SHÌT!

IT'S A SHAME YOUNGIN'
I know OLDHEAD'S
That Last Longer
THAN THIS

Put your Pride to the Side

Sit Back and ENJOY this Ride

This GROWN WOMEN might be

WHAT YOU BEEN MISSING INSIDE

FUCK AROUND

AND CHANGE YOU FOR A LIFETIME!

AND NOT ON NO COCKY SHIT

More like, have you up

You know that, ROCKY SHIT!

Have you on Top

We WON'T Stop, WE LIT

But you can't FUCK

A GOOD THING UP

Cause I'm on to the Next

Ella Ma Boo'd Up!

And Trust he Loving that Sweet
That Loud, that Gushy Stuff!
Wanting to Experiment
TIE ME UP ALL THAT GOOD STUFF

BUT NEVER FUCKING UP
So you Might Wanna Wish us
The Best of Luck!

Never Mad or In My Bag
Just Chucking my Deuces up
CAUSE I DON'T GIVE A FUCK!!

LOVE ♡

Grab me by the Hand

AND LEAD THE WAY

I wanna Remember EVERY Detail

About this SPECIAL DAY

The Room Lit Up from the Candles

And the Roses look like they were Placed

Perfectly, Pedal by Pedal

The Wine on Chill

And Music just above a Whistle

I know For a Fact after this Night

I'LL ALWAYS MISS YOU

Laid me Gently on the Bed

As I Caress and Rub my Hands

Around your Head

Opened My Legs
And your Eyes Lit Up
Like you Played the Lottery
AND HIT

Devouring me with EVERY Kiss
Not leaving ANYTHING to be Missed!!!
Looked up and Smirked, saying
Oh, how you Love my Hersey's Kiss

Melting away just from your Touch
How'd I get this Amazing man
IT MUST BE LUCK

Thrusting himself In and Out of me
Causing me to Gasp at every Hump
What did I do to Deserve
THIS SUPER EROTIC FUCK

Just being you, Beautiful and Sexy

Not leaving Room for ANYONE to Test me

I PRAYED to God about you

And it seems He finally Blessed me!

Soft Spoken and very Caring

I don't think NO ONE is ever coming Close

To COMPARING

STARING IN MY EYES

While we make Passionate Love

It's like we are Glued together

Like a FOREVER Hug

EVERLASTING IMPRESSION IS

EVERYTHING!!!

PERFECTLY FLAWED

Before you Judge me, Take a Walk

Down my Memory Lane

At age 10

That's when it all Began

The minute he Touched me

The PAIN Sunk in

Scared to tell the World

This GROWN MAN Touched me

Afraid what they would Say

And How they would JUDGE me

Not knowing this Shit

Would EVENTUALLY Fuck me

His Word AGAINST Mine

The World WOULDN'T Believe me,

So I Buried it Deep, NOT ALLOWING it to Hurt me

Didn't ANYBODY Notice?

Now at age 12, couldn't stop Peeping

That SHIT was Beyond me

But NOBODY would Speak!!!

Fast Forward Age 14

Now, I'm out here Grinding

Selling weed, working WHATEVER I had to do

To put that Time in

Sleeping on Friends Couches

Cause me and my little brother

Ain't have No House

And the One we did, the Lights Were Out

Pulling all-nighters out in the street

PRAYING TO GOD

Cause all we wanted to do was Sleep

Now, the Old heads are Noticing me,

Let me find out this young girl Popping

Nah, they were Clocking

Tryna see, who was gonna be the

First to put their Glock in

Silly me, young Dumb, and Ready for Fun

Giving all these niggas a TEST RUN

Meanwhile, the biggest drug dealer Won!

Hair stayed Done, always had a New Sneak

And people who I thought was my Friends

Only wanted to Smoke My Weed

Age 16 now, I'm in Survival Mode

Yeah, that Old Head he became Super Old

Time to Move On and get a New One

Now this Shit is Catching up to me

And I feel like I'm Done

Tired of the Lies and the same Reruns,

That Shit was really going In One ear

And Out the Other One!

Age 18, now I'm HEARTBROKEN

The Love of my Life has been TAKEN

At the Hands of ANOTHER MAN'S GUN

Now this PAIN here

Has LEFT ME NUMB!!!!

Time to Change my Life

Cause this Shit is No Longer Fun

Age 19, I thought I met the One

Not knowing this Battle

Would be My TOUGHEST ONE!!!

Physically and Mentally ABUSED

Whole-time, I was just being Used

Fool me once, I stayed

After that, CONTINUALLY Played

Like the Video Games, I paid for

Fuck that, now it's Time to EVEN THE SCORE

Moved on with my Life

Now it's like any Relationship

I want to ALWAYS End in Fight

Why I can't have what I want

And for Things to be Right

Guess that's why they call this Cruel World

COLD AS ICE

Stop Judging me OFF A PAST

You have No Idea About

Embrace the New and Improve me!!!

IM PERFECTLY FLAWED SO QUEEN ME...

MAKE YOUR BED

You Lay down and Have them

IT'S YOUR Responsibility to Take Care of him

Instead, you Run

I think it's the Fear in you

Growing up Fatherless

Has really done a Number on you

However, that child didn't have a Choice

So it should Open that Humble side of you!

You Remember being WITHOUT

SO IN RETURN

You should be there for yours

Without a Doubt

Your child's Mother didn't

Lay Down ALONE

And Carrying a child should already Show

She has NO CHOICE but to be Strong!

Restless Nights

While Working

And Providing on her Own

BARELY MAKING IT

But she REFUSES to Fold

Cause she has this Child

Y'all CREATED

But the MINUTE you Heard

YOU SKATED!

Missing FIRST Everything's

Those Memories are Worth Anything

Vice Versa, when they asked about their Dad

THEY DON'T REMEMBER

Cause he was NEVER a part of your Family Tree

Sad to say, it only his LOSS
Cause who's to say when these kids Grow
They WON'T be his Boss!

Nothing GOOD comes to a Man
Who doesn't RAISE his Child
Only God can mend the Hurt
And Hope the Child SURVIVES

FATHERLESS CHILDREN
Are like BUTTERFLIES
Before they get their Wings

But they Turn Out Beautiful
IN THE END!!

ME!!!

Nighttime is when

I become the Best Thinker

Blessed, Highly Favored

And DEFINITELY a Keeper!

Proud of my Growth

No matter, if anyone else Sees

And that's WITHOUT Seeking Help

From Someone Professionally!

Something in me Screamed

SET ME FREE!!!

Because I don't ever want to be in

That NEGATIVE SPACE that Consumed Me!

Living for Myself and NO in between

Not letting ANYONE OR ANYTHING

Control Me!

Let Your Soul Be Free

And you too WILL BE Thanking me

Cause being Happy will have you

Remove ALL NEGATIVITY!

POSITIVITY SPEAKS TO ME!!!

MOTIVATION

Saying all the Right Things is OK

But ACTIONS SPEAK LOUDER

And because of it, My Heart is Here to Stay

You Spoil me with Whatever

And you Try your Best

To Please my EVERY Need

When all I EVER WANT is your Time

You give me that on the Regular

And for me, that's Just Fine

I can NEVER get Enough of you

That's how I KNOW this Love

I have for you, is True

Every time I Think of You

I get that AMAZING Feeling

Like I POPPED a Pill or Two

That Feeling you get
After some EXPENSIVE Wine
That Feeling You Wish Could Last
FOR A LIFETIME

The CHEMISTRY is on Point
And the SEX is as Good as
The 2 Dimes stuffed in a Joint

ON CLOUD NINE
But Smiling like the SUNSHINE
God knows you ain't got to be this Fine
And to think this Man is Literally All Mine!

I give you ALL of me Leaving NO Room
For Mishaps or Anyone to Compete,
As long as you Continue to
ALWAYS RESPECT ME

Never having to Second Guess

Or Question Your Decision

Cause I give you My Word

You FILLED that position

Playing Your Part

Was just Half the Fight

Putting up with me was a Struggle

Cause I'm a DYNAMITE

Always ready to EXPLODE

But the Minute You Touch Me

I LOSE CONTROL

THAT SHIT YOU GOT

Is really Liquid Gold

I WILL NOT FOLD

OR EVER LOSE HOLD

Cherish when you have Someone

Or Something Special

Might be the MISSING PIECE

To Your SHATTERED PUZZLE!!!! ❦

ONLY ONE

You only get One

And I suggest you Cherish her

Cause WITHOUT her

YOU WOULDN'T EXIST!

To LOSE Her and NOT RESPECT Her

Is too much of a Risk

And that's not a Chance

I WILLING TO COMMIT

Brought you into this World

And WILL DEFINITELY Take You Out

Better Believe those Words

WITHOUT A DOUBT

She is One of the STRONGEST

People on Earth

So you Treat her with EVERYTHING

She's WORTH

ANYTHING LESS
Will cause NOTHING but Hurt!

Carried you for Nine Months
Pushed for hours during Labor
Anything she ASKED of you
Shouldn't ever be Considered a Favor

I couldn't Imagine Life WITHOUT her
And don't ever wanna get used to
THE THOUGHT EITHER

I COMMEND
Whoever has Lost their Mother

Cause that's HEARTBREAK, I can't Take
I'LL LOSE MY MIND
AND I'LL DEFINITELY BREAK!

Our everyday Conversations
And the Bond we Share
I give her FLOWERS
WHILE SHE'S HERE

Purple is our Favorite Color
And We have the SAME HEART
Some people can't even
TELL US APART!

Always been Inseparable
And I have NOTHING
But thee UPMOST RESPECT for you!

I'm my Daddy's Daughter
BUT FOREVER
My Mommy's Baby!!!

THANK YOU FOR CREATING YOUR LEGACY
Queen B!!!

P***Y TALK

Super Soaker 3000

That's what he Use to Call Her

Wasn't sure if he should Swim, Sink

OR RUN FOR COVER!

Couldn't GET ENOUGH

So he had NO CHOICE

But to SPOIL Her

Kissed her ALL Over

And DEVOUR by the End

Guess he felt like Mike Tyson

AFTER EVER WIN!

The MORE my Legs Shake

THE HARDER HE GO

And that Shit Drove me CRAZY

Every time he went EXTRA SLOW

In Tune with my Body
Like it was his FAVORITE HOBBY
Had me YELLING like I was Whitney
I LOVE YOU, BOBBY!!!

Got me Wanting to A STAND
LIKE I'M SOMEBODY!
Feeling like Beyoncé
When she sings, Get Me Bodied!!!

Throw that ASS in a Circle
He got me calling him papi!
LOSING CONTROL
While he calls out get it mami

Ecstasy on a NEW LEVEL
Or either this nigga was the devil
Cause ain't NO WAY IN THE WORLD
He got me SCREAMING
Like I'm singing A-cappella

READY SET START

The Hardest part is getting STARTED

But once you START

YOU'RE WANNA GO HARDER

Better than the Time Before

Shooting for a Perfect Score

ON A SCOREBOARD!

Never wanting to fail

so you give everyone hell

NOT INTENTIONAL

But with the Hopes of High Potential

Reaching Your Goal is your Only Mental

STAY ON TASK

So you NEVER come in Last

Show these people you got the LAST LAUGH!

Don't let their Opinions
From your PAST, get you Mad
Cause they GONNA WISH
THEY NEVER HAD

Strive for Success
And you Know the Rest
And KEEP all them Fake People Away
WHEN YOU'RE AT YOUR BEST!

They WASN'T Around
When you thought you were Gonna Drown
Look How Life
HAS TURNED AROUND

You're all the Way Up
And it's NOT cause of Luck
YOU STUCK TO YOUR GUNS
And got the JOB DONE

Life from Here On Out

Should be NOTHING but Fun

Your HARD WORK had Paid Off

AND YOUR LIFE JUST BEGUN!

Sometimes we DON'T want

That LONG TERM THING

We're just Looking for a

One Night Fling

Got to be BOLD about it

Cause some people

DON'T KNOW about it!

They might want More

and for you, that's a Bore

SO JUST MAKE IT CLEAR

BEFORE you decide to Explore

This Could Be what you Want

AND SO MUCH MORE!

Gotta be Willing to take that Chance tho

But if you LOVE HARD

IT'S DEFINITELY A NO GO!

Some do things Outta Spite

And others

Just Aren't That Type

Set BOUNDARIES in the Beginning

Or Your QUICKIE will for sure be

A BAD ENDING!!!

VALUE YOURSELF OR GET QUICKIE

WHICHEVER, KNOW YOUR WORTH!

SIDE HOP!

If it ain't Close Friends and Family

I GIVE UP

A lot of y'all be Fake and Phony

AND I DON'T GIVE A FUCK

PLAYING BOTH SIDES

Acting like you Gone Ride

But the MINUTE Shit Get Real

You Run and Hide!

You SUPPOSED to be my Homie

But you AIN'T Showing Up for Me

Instead, you having Side Bars

WIT THIS NIGGA JOEING ME!

What part of the GAME is that

YOUR LOYALTY IS WEAK!

I could care less if we ever,

Talk Again or Speak

I'm not saying NO PEACE

Or Playing for Keeps

Cause I know my Real Friends and Family

WE SQUAD WE DEEP!

SMOKING GUN

Ready to Pop Off

AND DON'T CARE WHO'S INSIGHT

All I know is it's TIME TO FIGHT!!

Pull up to ANY Scene

And grab my Pipe,

Don't Step OUTTA LINE

Cause I'll PULL WITH ALL MY MIGHT

For My LOVE

I'LL TAKE YOUR LIFE

Catch me at the Airport

Ready to Catch the NEXT FLIGHT

The thoughts of My Loved Ones Hurting

Is a FEELING I can't Control

It's no way IN HELL

I'm not bouta UNLOAD

Stand there and Watch

As their Body Folds

Now that FEELING right there

IS WORTH MORE THEN GOLD

Knew it was a Matter of Time

Before the Truth Be Told

Just a Bunch of Liars

Selling ANYTHING that can be Sold

It's three sides to EVERY STORY

Mines, Yours, and Now the Juniors

Only I can Speak My Story

So it's only Right, I'll be My Own Lawyer!

ALWAYS STAND YOUR GROUND NO MATTER

HOW MANY FROWNS YOU COME ACROSS!!

SOULFUL NOISE

Shivers ALL OVER, Biting My Bottom Lip

While putting my Hands around your Throat

Cause Your Grinding My Body

WITH THAT SUPER STROKE

MY MIND PACING, MY HEART RACING

YELLING PLEASE STOP

I CAN NOT TAKE IT!

Whole-time you Putting your Face in it

Slow Licking and Finger Sticking

I have NO CHOICE

BUT TO TAKE THIS SHIT!

You Studying MY EVERY MOVE

Like you're Studying for a Test

Trying to Complete it

AT YOUR BEST

Not making ANY WRONG MOVES

While I Moan Yes!

You Reassuring me

YOU'RE NOT FINISH YET

Giving Me Time

To Catch My Breath

AND YOU KNOW THE REST!

Caressing my Entire Body

Gotta me like a young Hottie

Wanting to Grind to the Beat

FROM LOTTIE DOTTIE

Somebody Stop Me

Better yet, Pop me

Cause this GOTTA be a Dream

OR IS MY REALITY?

Keep 'em Guessing

So you AIN'T Stressing

Not EVERYBODY Deserve

To be a part of your Blessing!

THANKFUL

Drop to my Knees at ANY Given Moment

Just to let him Know

I'm so WORTHY of His Name!!!

For he Eased My Pain

The moment I cried Insane

FATHER, I NEED YOU

I NEED You to Show Me the Way

It has to be MORE to My Life

For all, I have ENDURED

I DESERVE BETTER

And EVERYTHING You Have In-Store!

I'm just Waiting on the Moment

I can ACTUALLY Release

And be at Peace

But in the Meantime

I'll CONTINUE to be the Blessing

That You NEED me to Be!

I feel like the CHOSEN ONE
The ONE You PERSONALLY picked
To deliver what Good I have
And this AMAZING GIFT!

You Lift My Spirits
Even when I'm Down,
Showing me how EVERYTHING
IN THE BLINK OF AN EYE
Can Turn Around!

I'M SO GRATEFUL
There NOTHING in Life that can REPLACE You!!
Father, You are what Keeps me Going
And it's Your Blood through my Veins
That Keeps me Flowing

FOREVER STRONG IN THE LORDS NAME!

THE BEAR TRUTH

Might not be what you Want

But it's DEFINITELY gonna be the Truth!

No matter how Harsh or how it's Reciprocated

YOU WILL GET ALL OF ME!

Super Blunt but Extremely Fun,

That friend EVERYONE talks about

Yeah, I'm the ONE!

You call, I'll come with NO HESITATION

And NO SECOND GUESSING

All I need to hear is the Words

And you Looking Like You're STRESSING!

I'll Fight ANY BATTLE, Big or Small

IT'S ALL FOR ONE AND ONE FOR ALL!

Ask Me Anything

And I'm gonna tell it, Raw

NOT LOSING ANY SLEEP
Cause the next person Thinks
I'M GOING OVERBOARD!

I can't FAKE who I am
Or be Untrue!
That's like Telling you the SKY is Pink
WHEN WE ALL KNOW ITS BLUE

Born with all Brothers,
NO SISTERS for a Reason,
Never been the Type
To take ANYTHING Easy

So much Hurt in My Life
Not too many people I know
That can FIGHT THIS FIGHT!

I'm Stronger Than I Look
With an EVEN MEANER Left Hook,
Put ANYBODY in Front of Me
I can READ 'em like a Book

Always had Street Smarts,
And a Hustler Ambition
BUT BEING AROUND MY FAMILY
Is the ONLY THING that Softens My Heart!

My Mind STAYED on a Mission
Like I worked in the Kitchen
Through all my Struggles
I just knew I must Deliver!

Show the World my HIDDEN TALENT
Cause on Most Days
I COULDN'T LIVE WITHOUT IT!

NEVER GIVE UP ON YOU!

THE WORKING MAN

I'll take the 9 to 5

ANY DAY

Overdoing a Dime

One thing I don't like

IS WASTED TIME!

YOU STAY OUT ALL DAY

And INSTEAD of Coming Home

You decide to GO PLAY!

WHY DO YOU THINK IT'S OK

TO TREAT ME THAT WAY?

Like me being Loyal is NOT ENOUGH

I do EVERYTHING you say

Always wanting to be

THE HIGHLIGHT YOUR DAY!

Now You're Booked, and I Sit Back and Replay
All the Shit you did and your Ugly Ways
Now it's safe to say
You do know TWO CAN PLAY?

I'm not making NO VISITS
Or PUTTING My Life On Hold
Cause you knew that Block Life
WAS GETTING OLD!

You're in a Cell COLD
AND ALONE!
You want me to Except a Collect Call
NAH NIGGA, YOU BOLD

You DIDN'T Answer me
On all them Lonely Nights
Why do you think I Care to Fight?

You took ADVANTAGE of Someone
You CLAIM you Love
But out in Public
COULDN'T EVEN GET A HUG!

Type Time you was on
Oh Yeah, I was only there for Convenience
Now look who Stuck
Should've thought of the Consequences
BEFORE YOU FAKE ASS GENIUS!

Thinking with your LITTLE PENIS
Is what caused this Whole Hate
BETWEEN US

You Open My Eyes
And I FINALLY Realize
I'll take a Real Man
WHO WORKS 9 TO 5!!

TRUE BLESSINGS

My Rainbow Babies, that's what I call them

Never thought I'd see the Day

At least, that's what the Doctor's Would Say!!!

Ectopic Pregnancy and Serval Miscarriages later

To say it's a Girl and a Boy

Who fills me with SO MUCH JOY!!!

A rich man Dream

But an even BIGGER Dream for a Queen

Now I feel COMPLETE from Something

That was Taken Away from me

Not Once, Not Twice

BUT THREE TIMES I SCREAMED!

Praying for a Miracle

And I received DOUBLE THE BLESSING!

My Star and My Ace
I couldn't ask for a better Dynamic Duo
MY TWO LITTLE HEROES
That keeps me going and above Ground Zero!

Perfect Little People
With NO CARE in the World
The way kids should be
In this CRUEL CRUEL WORLD

Protect them as Long as you Shall Live
Cause WITHOUT them, Life just as is
Meaningless with NO PURPOSE
NO HOPE, JUST WORTHLESS!

They are so Special
And should be Treated as Gold
Cause ain't no telling
If they will see you Get Old

Cherish EVERY Moment
And Create AMAZING MEMORIES
Cause one day they'll be Talking about
All the GOOD THINGS they Remember!

Raise them Right
Teach them all the Lessons
They will NEED to Fight in Life

Give them Faith and Instill some type of Belief
Teach that it's OK to Pray on Bending Knee!
And Teach them in Life
THAT COMMUNICATION IS KEY!!

MOMMY LOVES YOU, TAYLOR & AYCE

UNBEARABLE

The Day I got that Call

Was the Beginning of the End

Lord, I begged You, NOT AGAIN!

But with this UNBEARABLE FEELING

I knew it Within

Why not me?

For I've have SINNED

They changed their ways

AND WAS TRYING TO WIN

Why my Kin Lord

I SCREAMED OUT LOUD

Blocking Every Word

That came out that Doctors Mouth

My Heart SNATCHED OUT my Chest

AS WE LAID NOT ONE

BUT TWO TO REST

Leaving me to Question
HOW GOD KNOWS BEST?

You take GREAT Souls
And Leave us here to Rot and get Old
It looks like; You took the Ones that Gold
And Put the Rest On Hold

The World is so Cruel and so Cold,
Sometimes I RATHER Be with You
TRUTH BE TOLD

But then, I Hear their Voices
And that's some Reassurance
Not only were they my Brothers
They were my Best Friends

Teaching me Right from Wrong
And Wrong from Right
Never allowing me to Break a Nail
OR EVEN TO FIGHT

Keeping me Sheltered and Out of Sight

No man was ever GOOD ENOUGH for me

NO MATTER HOW NICE

Treated like A Queen

Was an UNDERSTATEMENT

No one could EVER Fill that Bond

OR EVER REPLACE IT

My Brothers, My World,

Nothing in between

They are LITERALLY MY EVERYTHING

As I continue to Scream,

I LOVE YOU GUYS!

UNTIL THE DEATH OF ME!!!

Keep Me Covered and In Your Hearts! ✌

✓ Queen Elizabeth ♡

UNFORGETTABLE

15 YEARS LATER and it STILL seems like

We just saw each other Yesterday

It's Crazy, but they Say

GOD WORKS IN MYSTERIOUS WAYS!

To be out of My Life so long

And to Come Back

And the Feeling be so Strong

It's like the PERFECT Love Song!

Talk about a History

How we're STILL Living

Some days are a MYSTERY

We were Daredevils

Did nothing but STAYED IN TROUBLE

Had ANGELS WATCHING over us

Many times

Life was OVER FOR US!

We shared GREAT TIMES
We shared SAD TIMES
But through it all,
We REMAINED STRONG!

OUR WORD IS DEFINITELY A BOND
And OUR LOVE is Worth a LIFETIME

REAL LOVE DON'T DIE...

WITH OR WITHOUT

When We're Together

It's NO BETTER FEELING

Like ALL MY WORRIES

Have come to a Healing

Causing me to Develop

These CRAZY FEELINGS!!!

Feelings I CAN'T Explain

But not Questioning or Daring to Complain

It's an AMAZING Emotion

And it's DRIVING ME INSANE

I rather have this Happiness

Over any Kind of Pain!!!

Leaving me to Wonder

DO YOU FEEL THE SAME?

Some days are Good

But others are Unexplained

Like, do you Want Me To Be ALL IN?

Or Do you wish for me to REFRAIN?

We talk about EVERYTHING and ANYTHING

Which leaves me with Doubt Tryna Understand

WHY YOU WANNA BE WITHOUT?

WITHOUT MY LOVE,

WITHOUT MY ENERGY,

WITHOUT MY DEDICATION

AND TOTAL SUPPORT

It's supposed to be You and Me

AGAINST THE WORLD

Like we taking on a Whole Team

PLAYING FULL COURT!!!

Never wanna FEEL Alone

While being in your Presence

That's like GETTING to Paradise

BUT TURNED AWAY at the Gates of Heaven

Like having a FULL Buffet

With NO MOUTH TO EAT

This LOVE I have for you

MAN, THIS SHIT RUN DEEP!!

It's Like having a Closet Full of Sneaks

With NO FEET

BOY, THIS SHIT HERE IS SUPER STEEP!!

May I Repeat,

This LOVE I have for you

MAN, THIS SHIT RUN DEEP!!!

Deep enough to Know

I NEVER WANNA go Seek

Seek the ATTENTION of another Man

Especially when he's Weak

You're the ONLY MAN I SEE

And the ONLY ONE FOR ME

I Love you to the Sky, the Sun, the Moon

And the End of the Sea!!!

May I Repeat,

This LOVE I have for you

MAN, THIS SHIT RUNS DEEP!!!

It was your SMILE

That Attracted me to you

But it was the LOVE for your Mother

THAT MADE ME FALL IN LOVE WITH YOU

Not knowing that would be

THE DOWNFALL IN YOU

Years in the Lies became the Normal

And the INFIDELITIES I became Accustomed to

The Bad ALWAYS OUTWEIGHED

THE GOOD

But that I Overlooked

IN HOPES OF CHANGING YOU

NOT KNOWING

I was only Changing Myself

While DESPERATELY wanting to seek Help

To Embarrassed and Afraid of
THE I TOLD YOU SO'S
Keeping EVERYTHING Bottled up
CAUSE I FELT SO LOW

CRYING OUT for a Release
But NOBODY knows!!!
PLEASE, SOMEBODY, HELP ME
I'M ABOUT TO EXPLODE!

LOVE is a Beautiful Thing
But it's Something only a woman
With a DREAM has seen

The Perfect Life
A Perfect Wife
Yet, I'm sitting here
With a HEART OF ICE

I Pray for Happiness

So my Soul can be FREE AGAIN

And the LOVE I have for a New Man

CAN FINALLY BEGIN!!

Patience and Constant Persistence

Is the Way of Life

And now, I FINALLY have

A NEW INSIGHT

YOUNG QUEEN

Slow Down YOUNG QUEEN

You're MOVING too Fast

Only thing dude really wants

IS A PIECE OF YOUR ASS

They are Waiting to See

Who can get it First

Don't FALL FOR THE TRAP

It's just a Puddle of Thirst!

You're WORTHY of the World,

Don't let NOBODY tell you Different

You were Put on this Earth

To COMPLETE a Mission

Not to be Held Down

But to DEFINITELY

TO EXCESS!

You can Conquer the World
And DO ANYTHING you Put Your Mind to
Just STICK TO THE GOAL like Hot Glue
And watch how EVERYTHING COMES TRUE!

NEVER COMMIT TO ANYTHING
Unless it's MARRIAGE
Wish SOMEBODY would've told me
Then I wouldn't be so EMBARRASSED

Fight for your Goals,
And Stand for EVERYTHING you Believe in
NEVER GET DEFOCUS
Because that's when the devil SEEKS IN!

There will be MANY Distractions
But it's up to you to TAKE ACTION
Fight with Everything in you
Cause this is your PASSION!

NEVER GIVE UP
AND NEVER STOP TRYING
Because there's People Watching
And it's all about TIMING!

FOCUS, FOCUS, FOCUS,
These Boys will come Later
Do EVERYTHING you Need to Do
So you can SMILE for your HATERS!!!

Slow up BEFORE it's too Late,
Take your Time, and you'll see
That thing called LIFE is a Beautiful Place!

Set the TONE for
ALL YOUNG QUEENS around the World
I was ONCE that Little Girl
With NOTHING to Look Up To!

ZAID

I NEVER questioned Allah,

But this Pain here, Hurt!

Secrets you took to your Grave

BUT I WISH YOU COULD BE SAVED

Best Father I know

Beautiful Smile and an Amazing Glow!

My Motivation and Light

When EVERYONE else said NO

WHY YOU?

That's all I keep Thinking

Got that call

And my Heart INSTANTLY began Sinking!

Felt like I couldn't Breathe

ALL OVER AGAIN

Like someone was Sticking Deep Within!

This Feeling NEVER GOES AWAY
I Wish on ANY Given Day
YOU WERE HERE
But that COWARD will Pay!

CAN'T BRING MYSELF TO GO
To the Place, you Lay
All I can do is Hope and Pray!

My Motivation is Gone
And HASN'T Been the Same
When EVERYONE Turned their Back
YOU REMAIN THE SAME

NEVER on NO DISRESPECTFUL Type
You wanted all your Clients to Shine!
Damn, I wish I could REWIND
THE DAYS AND TIME!

WE MISS YOU DOWN HERE ZAID

And I PROMISE to make you Proud

I'll NEVER Stop

AND I'LL NEVER LOOK DOWN!!!

ABOUT THE AUTHOR

Shakeya Kinard is a lifelong writer, but currently, she is a new author. Shakeya was born and raised in Wilmington, Delaware, best known by most as the First State, the place to be somebody!

Delaware is very small, but it is known for its high crime rate and no tax law.

Daughter of Mother Jackie Kinard, and Father Walter Miller, and loving Stepfather Kelly Harrison. The only girl raised in a household full of brothers, cousins, and uncles.

Shakeya grew up on the mean streets on the West Side of Wilmington, which most people call the best side! Where legends were born. She Attended the Red Clay school district most of her adolescent years and later Graduated from Glasgow high school.

In addition to Coaching Majorette and Juicing, Shakeya is a proud mother of two children. It Wasn't until after high school that the love for writing consumed Shakeya's life, keeping hundreds of diaries and thousands of notes!

Writing has always been a passion but seeing her work published is a dream come true. Growing up, her parents always had high expectations of her, and at the age of 35, she now feels she has delivered.

Being the first to become a self-published author is major for our family. But it's also the start of many more Amazing Accomplishments!

CPSIA information can be obtained
at www.ICGtesting.com
Printed in the USA
LVHW031444261120
672639LV00003B/312